the
healing
you
hear

the healing you hear

For Rusty

Table of Contents

Preface

Grateful, aligned, and embracing opportunities that came from obedience—I couldn't ask for more. It was a winning season. I stepped out on faith, discovered a new path on my spiritually led move, and found myself living a life that had long time been prayed, promised, and prepared for.

Everything was falling into place, new and exciting. Yet with that feeling of adventure and realization that I was no longer in alignment with my familiar scenery or routine, there came a strong awareness and weight of what didn't belong. I got sick.

My mind, body, and spirit reacted. Medical test results and spiritual wisdom confirmed that my body was not simply *acting* differently. It was reacting and rejecting me because it was constantly preparing for stress, as well as suppressing what wasn't mine to hold.

For much of my life, suppressing my emotions, observing instead of reacting, pleasing people, and aiming to be *good* made me feel like the bigger person, the strong friend, the dependable one, and a more empathetic person.

Eventually, pushing my feelings and needs aside made me a shell of myself. It turned me into the person who invalidated and abandoned me the most. It made my body reject itself, leading me to resent others. It caused me to struggle with being fully present. I was surrounded by light; but, I struggled to embrace the warmth and beauty of it all. I was walking in purpose, grateful, and happy while a part of me felt like I was performing. I always felt I was carrying something that didn't belong.

Coming to this realization led me to understand that I not only needed to dive deeper within myself and my faith but also needed to release all that weighed on my heart, mind, and spirit for so long. I had to audit my thoughts, accept my experiences, and name the emotions behind them while giving myself permission to be a safe place within myself to release it all. I gave myself permission to love and celebrate myself; lean on and confide in others, and speak and be seen without fear.

I had to hold myself accountable, articulate what I tried to ignore, and have both difficult and healing conversations with others. At the same time, I had to have honest and validating conversations with myself. It was time to finally see and show up for myself in a way I never had before. I had to hear my own voice and fully appreciate the person I am and every step of the journey that led me here.

As you turn each page, read each word, and embrace every emotion expressed, I encourage you to speak this collection of poetry and prose out loud.

Allow yourself to hear and recognize the pieces of your journey that connect and the lessons that have the power to lead you to healing, understanding, and acceptance of who you are and the journey you continue to travel. Give yourself permission to also acknowledge, articulate, and alleviate yourself from what no longer serves you and the innermost thoughts that hold you back.

I see you, hear you, and understand you. Now, you must do it for yourself.

It's time to turn the page on your life's pain and begin writing a new book filled with the expectation of joy, alignment, and transformation that came from it all.

Introduction

There will come a season of your life where your healing will lead you to growth, peace, and awareness you never experienced before. You will be aligned with a level of safety and conviction that will expose every survival tactic, strength, and suppressed emotion you safeguarded within.

You will be grateful yet grieving; healing yet hurting. Your body will react, your mind will remember, and your spirit will crave a release that not only renews your sense of self but also reminds you of the power and authority that resides in your voice.

To fully experience the peace that is only found in release and heal the voice and relationship you have with your innermost self, you must wholeheartedly **accept** every experience and emotion you've endured. Give your mind, body, and spirit permission to process every part of your path and every chapter of your journey.

You must **speak** what you once suppressed, validate your own emotions and experiences, and have conversations that bring you clarity and closure.

By releasing and reframing your pain, remembering your worth, and realigning with your purpose, you can finally **live** in the peace and power that comes from accepting your authentic self and honoring all that you are.

At some point, we will not be able to convince ourselves that we let go of, processed, or made peace with something if we didn't. We will not be able to pretend that we truly love, respect, and accept ourselves if we aren't there yet either.

Because what our mouths do not say our thoughts, nervous system, reactions, and spirit will echo within us.

Sometimes we allow all that we can't undo, can't control, or can't accept to become our innermost voice, insecurities, and identity. Because our hurt is often louder than our healing.

But honoring our healing, embracing who we truly are, and accepting the greater purpose of every path of our journey changes everything. Putting in God's hands what we were never meant to carry frees us of a weight and allows us to move forward mentally, spiritually, and emotionally.

It allows us to see, hear, and process *what is* while having hope for *what can be*. It is reflected in the words we speak, the energy we emit, and all that we give our attention to.

We advocate for ourselves and respect the discernment reminding us that though it is foolish to cast our pearls before swine, there will come a time when it's necessary to speak. There will be seasons and situations where our voice is the key to our closure and our well-being.

Therefore, use conviction not to condemn but to correct yourself and cultivate your strength—so you can confidently continue your life with peace, clarity, and acceptance of who you are. You set the tone for your life, mind, and healing.

Be the voice you need to hear and the person you no longer silence.

the healing you hear

ACCEPT IT

It happened.
It isn't happening.

You are safe. The storm is over.

You are no longer in the season where you pray God helps you handle the pain. This is the season you ask God to help you properly manage and embrace joy.

Your inability to let go of the past was never tied to weakness or immaturity. It was always related to the fact that it needed to be the right time and a safe season to do so. A season, environment, and space in your life where you could unpack, feel, and process every path in your journey up to this point.

A level of healing where you can finally verbalize all that lay dormant within you and talk about all that you mentally reference yet never released.

You do not have to rush the process, but you must respect it.

This part of your healing journey was waiting until you were ready. And now you are.

You are not going to be the same.

You are not going back to being the person you were before.
Before it all hurt. Before that time in your life.
Before you experienced the memory of the past that just
reappeared in your mind.

And as dark as that statement may seem, the truth remains that
you truly will not give yourself permission to feel the light until
you acknowledge the darkness.

Until you realize your aspiration from this point on should not be
pursuing and regaining the normalcy or naivety you once had.

The journey now requires you to press forward with healing your
innermost wounds and no longer mentally holding yourself
hostage with what hurts you so deeply.

I was not able to heal, release, or fully forgive my pain
until I accepted that I was truly hurt.

Until I accepted that those experiences impacted me far longer
and deeper than I ever articulated or even understood at the time.

Until I made peace with the fact that holding on to the offense,
resentment, and unforgiveness towards others and myself was
not only robbing me of my inner peace but also creating a
breeding ground for bitterness, anger, and depression.

There is a process to processing—yet we do not give ourselves
the time, compassion, or grace to realize that profound truth.

Until we accept the presence of our pain, we cannot honestly and
wholeheartedly create an exit strategy to release it.

Healing is a journey.
You owe it to yourself to take every step.

Instead of dwelling, seek to dive into the piece of yourself that is desperate for healing. The piece of yourself that is ready to move forward in forgiveness, peace, and wisdom.

Give yourself permission to process. Prepare yourself to release the mental, spiritual, and emotional weight you've been carrying for far too long.

Internalizing and intellectualizing—the language many *healing while hurting* people have grown accustomed to.

Infused with innermost thoughts, emotions, insecurities, experiences, and the mental tug of war between emotional maturity and human psychology, we so often struggle to discover true peace because we do not give ourselves permission to process at all.

We are grieving yet grateful, set free yet feeling stuck, and walking in faith while being pulled down by what we can't forget—processing the past while actively trying to live in and appreciate the present.

It's a balancing act and battlefield in the mind reminding you that the burdens you refuse to break free from and the truths you have yet to speak are the very obstacles throwing you off course.

You pride yourself on being open-minded and empathetic towards others, yet you judge yourself for the ways in which you navigate pain and question your own faith and emotional intelligence for feeling anger, feeling unheard, or struggling with unforgiveness.

You instantly try to look for the positive instead of giving yourself a safe place to land in the present moment. Trying so badly to identify the blessings in negative experiences that you don't acknowledge the magnitude of the burdens those very experiences brought. Battling between how you believe you should feel and reacting with the truth of how it affected and changed you.

Truth is, trying to get rid of anger is actually creating more. It is building frustration and fixation on the fact that you can't seem to break free from a pain you've grown familiar to feeling and suppressing.

No matter how much you try to cover all the ways it cripples and constricts you—or overcompensate with affirmations and inner work—the base of this burden is simple.

Underneath it all, it's hurt.

It's unexpressed, undeniable, and unshakable hurt that seems to cycle.

You feel unseen, you become overly protective of yourself, and fearful to experience anything that could break or scar your heart again. There is a void. You feel violated and voiceless yet push it away instead of processing.

Healing is nonlinear and often misunderstood—even by the person actively pursuing it. It's a process that lightens the yoke you've been carrying, but only after making it painstakingly aware how heavy it has become.

It will lead you to see the fruits that conditioning, stress, and confusion have had on your actions and reactions. You will be led on a journey to discover and dissect the mental, spiritual, and emotional roots behind them.

They are still your pieces to pick up,
even if you didn't break them.

It's time to stop waiting on someone else to step in, step up, and
save the day.

It is your responsibility to heal from any hurt that hinders you.

What happened may not have been fair.
What happened may have occurred years ago.
What happened may not have been your fault.
What happened may have been at the hands of your former self.

What happened, happened.
Now, you must put yourself together again.

The apology and acknowledgment you were waiting for—speak
it to yourself. The emotions that you suppressed because you
were scared to let them out—name and release them.
The support and validation you prayed for—extend to yourself.

You will either continue to crawl in circles as you mentally
rewind and replay the pain and struggles of your life, or you will
finally face it head on as you walk out of your internal
suffering—no matter how foreign those steps may be.

The choice is and will forever be yours.

It's the grey that gets me.

The grey areas in my life where I spent so much time trying to understand the whys within myself.

Why did this happen?
Why did I react that way?
Why didn't I do more?
Why didn't I remove myself?
Why did I put myself in that situation?
Why do I still wrestle with this?
Why didn't I do better?
Why did I accept that?
Why do I think and feel this way?
Why am I so stuck in the whys?

And although this persistent need to understand and address myself has led to growth and maturity, it has also led me to question myself in times I should have stood firm on what I knew.

It led me to condemn and criticize myself so brutally that I forgot how to give myself grace when I was met with confusion or show myself love when I felt lost.

I can hold myself accountable without becoming my own mental aggressor. I can extend compassion to myself as I connect the dots of my life and mindset.

The Weight of Why

There's a weight I've carried in the center of my chest
that has only dragged me down over time.
A weight that changed so much about me;
yet, was never meant to be mine.

It came from not speaking up
because I didn't feel safe—
holding on to projections
instead of letting them fall away.

Instead of acting out of character
or casting my pearls before swine,
that pain you threw at me, I picked up
and somehow made it mine.

Maybe you wouldn't have said that
if you actually knew the truth.
Maybe I deserve to be treated that way,
though I'd never do that to you.

Now, years later, I catch myself not breathing,
taking these long and winded sighs.
You sit back and judge my silence
but never cared to ask or understand the reason why.

Accepting the *what is*
of your pain is where healing begins,
not understanding *the why*
of the person who inflicted it.

Maybe what was supposed to happen never did.

Maybe the support that was supposed to be there for you never came. Maybe the part of you that expected the best overall outcome was shattered when you realized life isn't fair.

There comes a point when you must acknowledge all that transpired and all that didn't.

A point where you give yourself the love, compassion, and strength needed to move forward with the acceptance of what is and what was, so you live fully in what is to be.

You may never forget those times you cried.

Those times you cried yourself to sleep to the point where you woke up with puffy eyes. Those times you cried as you ate dinner and tears flowed into your plate. Those times you cried in the bathtub and wished you could wash your pain away.

You may never forget those times. However, there will come a time when you must put it all behind you. Not in a way to ignore those seasons, struggles, and suffering you went through, but in a way that you give your mind, body, and soul permission to experience and expect joy again.

You give yourself permission to laugh until your stomach and cheeks hurt. You give yourself permission to be so excited about the next day that you can't sleep the night before. You give yourself permission to fully embrace the present and be excited about the future.

Tears will come...
but so will joy.

the healing you hear

I am not unaware of the weight you've been carrying. I understand just how much it has impacted your life. The pain, the pressure, the stress you feel in the pit of your stomach all seem so permanent right now.

I need you to reflect on and rest in the truth that those feelings won't last forever.

One day, all the hurt you were wrestling with will no longer haunt you or make you feel like you are mentally holding yourself hostage. There will come a time when walking in forgiveness and extending grace will feel more natural than sulking in frustration and holding on to grudges.

You will not only embrace the peace that comes with realizing you're not defined by the tests, triumphs, and traumas of your past but also be empowered by how far you've come. Though it is difficult to imagine right now, believe it.

The road to healing may not be easy, and the time frame may test your patience and faith. Faint not.

Healing is possible and available for you.

The relationship you have with yourself matters.

How you see yourself, speak to yourself, and show up for yourself sets the tone for your life, how you live it, along with who and what you align with and allow.

If you have more anger than acceptance, more shame than self-assurance, more condemnation than confidence, or more insecurity than authenticity—navigating the hills and valleys of life will be immeasurably difficult. Embracing joy and serenity will be met with caution instead of comfort.

Give yourself permission to feel your emotions without guilting yourself for having them or abandoning yourself to please others.

Healing changes the way you hear others,
the tone of your innermost thoughts,
and the words that come out of your mouth.

Sit with it.

Without trying to mentally manipulate the outcome of what's already done or rewriting the script of conversations you've already had.

Sit with it and accept it for what it was.
What's done is done.
No word spoken or choice made can be taken back. Neither can the memories of you suffering in silence or the tears crossing your face be undone.

Sulking in the could haves and should haves is draining you.
Looking back and realizing all you tolerated, all you did or didn't do, and all that was never okay is disgusting you.

Constantly dwelling on what happened is not healing you—it's distracting you, destroying your inner peace, and distancing you from your present state.

Feel it. Name it. Sit with it. Process it. Release it.
In time, the sadness you're sitting in
will become the strength you stand on.

I did more than care.
I carried.

I carried the burden of words, opinions, and the past around to the point where I forgot to live in the present. I harbored anger, resentment, and bitterness towards people who hurt me. This led me to not express my appreciation to those who helped me along the way or make myself available to new healthy relationships.

I dragged the shackles of condemnation around daily with the memories of my own ignorance, inaction, and issues.

I carried the baggage of yesterday until I realized that nothing within it was needed, aligned, or conducive to the growth of the person I am today.

So often, we spend years of our lives fixating on the dark clouds—plagued with anxiety, fearing the rain, and preparing for the storms—only to watch them pass us by and not be touched by a single drop.

Maybe it's because we endured emotional tornadoes that threw everything in our lives around and left us scrambling to pick up the pieces. Perhaps we wrestled in the waters of depression, where it took every ounce of our strength to keep our heads above each wave and rebuild everything that washed away.

But if we always fear and prepare for the disaster, how can we fully enjoy and find gratitude in the sun and all the light it carries?

There comes a point when we must stop being shaken by the possibility of struggles and keep our peace knowing we can withstand them.

The pain was real, but it is no longer current.

Now, with every ounce of your being, thought in your mind, and your faith rooted in God—you must pivot.

No longer will you dwell on what depressed you or replay the memories, details, and words that rattled your soul. No longer will you wait for the next painful experience to happen, your next misstep to be taken, or for someone to let you down.

MORGAN RICHARD OLIVIER

You see yourself as a vessel, yet you do not see the imbalance that comes from not allowing yourself to be nourished by all that you pour.

God does not give you a word, gift, or personality to merely love, enlighten, and uplift everyone *but* you.

Give yourself the space to hear and feel your own words and testimony. Give yourself the time to work through your own feelings and the compassion needed to carry on when you're ready.

You must make yourself available and hold yourself accountable when it comes to your own healing.

You've been there for everyone you love,
but now you must love and offer that to yourself.

You so desperately want to reach and help others with their baggage that you conveniently ignore the truth that you're still carrying baggage of your own.

A weight that has built your emotional intelligence and empathy but has bruised your sense of self and inner voice. It shows in the way you overthink every interaction, struggle to feel safe, and prepare yourself for disappointment—yet you are unwilling to speak to the fact that you were not always this way, nor do you have to be.

You don't have to sacrifice your sanity to keep the comfort of everyone around you. You don't have to silence your truth because you fear others will not believe, receive, or respect it. You don't have to become a shell of yourself because your wholeness intimidates the world.

The validation of every person you know means nothing if you can't validate, love, and support yourself.

The person who was holding you back is not a family member, friend, or someone you believe doesn't value you. The one who is holding you hostage and halting your healing journey is and always has been you.

Get out of your head. Get out of your own way.

This is your life. Take it back, face it head on, and live it unapologetically.

Jeopardizing your sanity because you're wanting the storm to just be over, seeking acceptance in familiar yet emotionally unsafe communities, and desiring peace so badly that you'll wreck your own nervous system, inner voice, and sense of trust sometimes says more about your inner fears, strongholds, and stress responses than your words ever could.

There are times when anxiety is obvious and unable to ignore.
It's that feeling when you lose your balance on a ladder—trying
to keep from going over the edge and you break into an instant
sweat. Shaking, self-soothing, and gasping for air like your lungs
are being squeezed out. Speaking from your mouth what your
mind can no longer contain. Racing thoughts, heart pounding,
and trapped.

And then there are times when panic is paralyzing.
There is no stuttering, heavy breathing, or cause for attention. It
feels like you're falling into your body—leaving you frozen,
unable to speak. Numb. Physically still yet emotionally shaken.
Mentally trying to pull yourself together yet falling apart. Your
heart is pounding, your thoughts are racing, and you're just there.

The world feels like it's crumbling around you,
yet most people around you have no idea.

Exhausted, empty; yet, still empathetic.
Showing up, smiling yet still stuck.
You're functioning yet frozen.

Time has moved on,
but your body and mind have not.

You're constantly anxious, operating while overwhelmed, and
accustomed to preparing for the worst but you don't have to. You
are mentally anticipating a battle, when there is no threat.

You are safe.
Now, you must heal, rest, and teach
your body to accept that truth.

When you're safe and settled,
the sickness will show.

Your body will bring to the top all that you buried within you.
Imbalances, inflammation, and fatigue will present themselves.
So will the realization that you were stuck in and no longer need
to be in survival mode.

Stress didn't just live in my mind.
It took residence throughout my body.

It stayed locked in my shoulders, twisted my stomach, and laid
heavy on my chest. It manifested and showed up as
inflammation, muscle tension, and a slew of ailments.

For the longest time, I couldn't understand or explain it.

We focus so much on healing the mind and strengthening the
spirit, that we ignore the importance of addressing the body—the
very place we often store trauma, fear, and stress. Our bodies
have a way of holding on to what we thought we let go of or
moved past.

You forget...
until you can't.

Until the brain fog, chronic fatigue, or inflammation refuses to
be ignored. Until someone says something, does something, or
you're triggered in a certain way. Suddenly, you're back in the
depths of the emotions you thought you'd left behind.

Until your body breaks the silence your mouth never did.

You ignore it until
it interrupts everything.

The problem with avoiding and not acknowledging your feelings is that they don't simply go away. They stay locked within you until the sentiment boils over and burdens your life or you give yourself permission to set it free.

Feel the hurt, allow yourself to cry until your body shakes. Make space to rest and reflect, and finally accept the truth that your emotions were always valid—and so are your needs.

Did you handle it well or did you simply not make your issue an issue for everyone else?

Did you handle it well or did you not speak up because you were struggling to process all you experienced and felt unsafe to share with those around you?

Did you handle it well or did you give yourself countless tasks to complete in an effort to occupy your mind and place your identity in accomplishments to overcompensate for the fact that you were lonely yet well received?

Did you handle it *at all*?

Suffering in silence, functioning through frazzled emotions, and showing up is not a sign that you are handling it well. Sometimes it is merely the proof that you are suppressing.

Yes, you handled it with maturity, strength, and integrity but now you must hand over all you carried within you, all that weighed you down, and all that is too heavy to bear over to God.

It happened—even if no one else knows it happened.
It happened—even if no one caught on, asked about it, or
supported you.

No matter how much you try to push the memory to the back of
your mind, no matter how much you try to avoid any
conversation remotely related to it—it happened.

And pretending that it didn't happen, didn't shake you, and didn't
lead you to change the way you view yourself, the world, and
everyone around you is not helping.

Suppressing is forcing you to keep those memories tucked within
your mind and trapped within your body.

Holding it in is only holding you back.

You can't redo, revise, or remove pieces of your journey out of
your life, but you can release the grip it has on you and its ability
to hinder you further.

That's the thing about seasons of life that shake you. The jilt not only confuses and overwhelms you, but it also rattles insecurities you thought you lost and digs up every emotion you thought was buried.

You are forced to come face-to-face with the worst or weakest version of yourself while making you aware of the person you were created to become is not unattainable.

It reveals the roots of your unrest, and if you're humble and ready to heal, it also reveals a greater purpose for every pain and path that leads to peace and power.

Lord, I need your words to echo in my mind louder than my own. I need your plans and hopes for me to persevere even if they do not align with mine.

I know what you have for me is exceedingly and abundantly more than I could ever imagine. But for me to obtain it, I must follow, obey, and live right by you.

Some people simply need a person they can be their authentic self with. A safe person who has love, compassion, and wisdom to give.

Although you may pride yourself on being that type of person for everyone around you, you must honestly ask if you are that person for yourself?

Do you give yourself room to process your experiences and emotions or have you created a mental prison to merely suppress or replay them?

Do you allow yourself to feel and let life flow, or are you so critical of yourself that you keep it all in and later condemn yourself for doing so?

At my worst, I craved being seen and heard so badly.

I craved the ability to delve into conversations without altering my vocabulary and learning about new perspectives and principles. I wanted people to be able to look into my eyes and see my soul. I wanted them to hear my voice and know how genuine the words I was speaking were. I wanted to be fully myself while not fully knowing who I truly was at the time.

I didn't place boundaries.
I placed barriers.

My fear of being hurt led me to hurt people.

It made me consistently inconsistent, unable to make myself
emotionally available fearing I wasn't safe. It encouraged me to
lead with silence at times when speaking would have set me free,
thus setting the standard of how I wanted to be treated.

Loving people yet not feeling safe around them is a unique pain many of us have experienced, yet few of us feel comfortable expressing.

It feels like being triggered into fight-or-flight when engaging with them. It sounds like the depth of your faith when you are praying and interceding for them.

It's a love that is genuinely felt within you but is best executed when they are not around you.

My initial response to disrespect or mistreatment was always to be nicer, be quiet, be the bigger person, and forgive as quickly as possible.

I thought reacting or responding would make it worse.

I thought I was keeping the peace, and in many ways, I was.
I was keeping the peace for everyone who brought chaos while creating a loud, long, and unforgiving war within myself.

A war that not only made it difficult to forgive or stand up for myself but also led me to mercilessly dilute my essence and silence my voice.

That moment of disgust when you realize and accept the truth that your painful silence and efforts to just let things pass only benefited those who purposely tried to destroy the peace and sanity within you.

Disgust for the times you should have cut people off without guilt and never looked back but instead you prayed tirelessly for them to see the truth and goodness within you.

Instead of accepting the revelation and motives within them, you question your own worth and all that you are.

Silence has come to be the safest and sweetest sound.

A subtle reminder that I am at peace, and everything connected to me is functioning and flowing as it should.

Solitude is about more than being selective or cultivating solace. In seasons of overwhelm, it has been my survival mechanism, shield, and a way to maintain my sanity.

It's my escape when I feel overwhelmed, unheard, misunderstood, or unable to manage.

It's the key that unlocks my creativity and opens my mind to greater perspectives, poetry, and the pieces of life that connect me to purpose.

It's a tool for revelation, giving me the opportunity to observe the behaviors and patterns of myself and others; one equipping me with wisdom.

Somehow, I always found myself trying to prove something. Whether it was my worth, my heart, or how it was valid for me to feel the way I felt.

Yet somehow you never had to do that with me.

You always knew I'd show up, liked the fact that I would carry and protect your emotions, expected me to understand, appreciated the love I showed, and didn't think twice to ask me anything.

Because I was the strong one, right?

The one who will figure it out. The one you don't have to worry about. The one you can depend on. The one who has their life together.

But if I'm all these things to you, then why do I constantly feel like I am not seen, heard, or understood by you? Why do I feel immense guilt when I say 'no,' share how I feel, do what's right for myself, or place a boundary?

Why am I so vocal when it comes to showing up for you yet silent when I have so much to say for myself.

The less I was understood, the more I overthought. The less I was appreciated, the more I overextended myself. The less I stood on the truth of who I was and the power of my authenticity, the more I fell for life's distractions and lowered my emotional standards.

As easy as it would be to point the finger at everyone I viewed as unappreciative or unable to reciprocate, I would have four fingers pointing back at me acknowledging that I did not have control over their actions, but I had control over my efforts and an unwillingness to remove myself from what was not aligned with my life.

It was no one else's fault that I wanted to be accepted in spaces where I was not aligned. It was no one else's fault that I could not validate myself, so I searched for the validation of my family and friends. It was no one else's fault that my inability to place boundaries and clearly articulate my emotions and experiences led to a suppressed and diluted version of myself.

If I want to break free from limiting thoughts, spiritual strongholds, and an unhealthy amount of insecurity then I must fully acknowledge the part I played in every single one of my life lessons.

Sacrificing her outer voice lowered her inner voice.
It gave negative self-talk a mic, her insecurities a foothold, and
made the words of others a hurdle.

She was an advocate, an empath,
and a sanctuary for everyone but herself.

She validated and made room for the world's
emotions but never her own.

the healing you hear

I resented myself for the things I didn't do,
the boundaries I did not set,
and the words I never spoke.

Whether that silence stemmed from wisdom,
obedience, stress, or discernment—it weighed on me.

There's something about carrying shame you didn't earn that has a way of making you sick to your stomach and boiling with anger that doesn't quite know how to seep out.

There's something about having a truth to tell and a point to prove yet having just enough discernment to know that sharing with people who are committed to misunderstanding you or unwilling to receive you will only make your internal battle and monologue worse.

So, you allow the words and the world around you to creep into your heart to attack your identity and ability to trust. So, you suppress everything and allow it to suffocate you.

Becoming bitter towards those you feel should know better and completely resentful towards the version of yourself that didn't.

Some of the worst mental and spiritual lies we will ever tell ourselves go to the tune of:

It will never get better.
I will always feel this way.
No one will ever understand me.
It will never be my turn.
There is no point in talking about it.

We allow our unmet expectations, unfulfilled time frames, and unaddressed pains to not only lead to prolonged states of doubt but also find ourselves unable to live in the present. We find ourselves stuck in past, bracing for further disappointment in the future.

It's a state of being that not only skews our view of life but also distorts our view of self.

What you say to people
can replay in their minds
like a broken record for years.

Be sure the words you speak
are kind, true, and centered in love.

The way others perceive you and how they choose to treat you —kindly or critically—you cannot control.

The tests and triumphs you endured and choices you made throughout your life—you can't change.

The damage or development done and the words spoken—you can't undo.

But when it comes to the emotions you felt, the experiences that shaped you, and the way those insights impacted you—you can accept.

The way people treat you is their choice.
It is not in your realm of control.

You can't make anyone value, support, or protect you who does
not want to. No matter the role you had in their life, how well
you treated them, or how long you've known them. All the
kindness, compassion, and care you extend will not guarantee a
person will have the capacity or desire to reciprocate any of that
to you.

And as difficult as that truth may be to accept, you must also
understand that what feels like rejection from people you love is
oftentimes God's painful yet profound gift of redirection. He's
highlighting the need for you to reevaluate your priorities and the
positions you currently have people placed.

the healing you hear

Sometimes the depth of your own thoughts
is the most dangerous place you can be.

Walking away from conversations only to later overthink and overanalyze everything has become your new normal.

Replaying everything you said, everything you didn't say, wondering if you talked too much or too little, if your tone was off, if they misunderstood your heart, or if you should have just stayed quiet altogether.

You say to yourself some variation of 'I hope they don't think...' then insert every possible worst-case scenario under the sun.

The fact that you leave a moment and then find yourself stuck in a mental loop to process, overanalyze, and come up with a plethora of ways you could have said or handled something that's already done is exhausting.

In your mind you try to please people who likely aren't thinking about past conversations anymore and protect yourself from misperceptions that likely don't even exist.

You know who you are. God knows who you are.
You do not have to punish yourself or become concerned about
what other people think or say.

You know your motives and exactly what you meant whether
they are properly perceived or not.

Even though you feel unsure and overthink, it does not mean you
are unsafe or unworthy of your own grace.

You do not have to carry the burden of perception, try to decode
the root of everyone's body language, or replay anything you
can't redo. It's okay to let it go, realign your focus, and simply be
yourself.

You are enough.

It's exhausting and even embarrassing to admit sometimes because I feel like I should be better and beyond that by now.

I feel like I have the tools, have learned the lessons, and gained a renewed mindset enough not to dwell on such things.

But if I'm honest—I still do.

I still struggle with imposter syndrome, negative self-talk, and other insecurities. Maybe it's because I'm mindful of my impact and obedience. Perhaps it's tied to still healing in real time.

I think it's important to note that no matter how much you advocate, empathize, or seek to leave a positive influence, you're still an imperfect person, work in progress, and worthy of your own compassion.

God, help me to release all that my mind routinely repeats.

Help me to focus on the parts of my lessons that built my character, faith, and wisdom. Free me from fixating on the burdens that came with them. Rewire my mind in a way that revels on greater purpose in all things and repels the desire to dwell on the principles.

You not only allowed every step of my journey, but use them to elevate my life and impact the lives of others.

Ever think back to the times you tolerated the absolute worst behavior from people yet guilted and shamed yourself into believing you somehow deserved it?

The empathy in you sought to understand the why and extend compassion to them, instead of accepting how it impacted you and what was truly going on.

Maybe your silence was wisdom, or maybe it was fear. But one thing is for sure, some of your silence was also the greatest ally for some people to escape accountability. Some of your silence served as the very lock that created a prison cell within your mind and convinced you that because you didn't use your voice you no longer had one.

It's the double-edged sword of healing.

Clearly seeing the violations and frustrations of the past yet acknowledging that you must heal from the hurt and release your silent suffering so you can experience peace in the present and future.

No amount of dwelling, replaying, or resenting
will take away the fact that it hurt.

How long are you going to stand in your shower replaying how
the conversation or situation should have gone? How long are
you going to hold on to anger, spike your cortisol levels, and
stop yourself from forming healthy relationships because you
can't get over what was?

It's the waiting that is wasting you away.

Waiting for fairness will leave you frozen in time.
Waiting for the next issue or disappointment is what's keeping
you worried. Waiting on all that isn't in your control only
distracts you from giving your time, energy, and attention to
what is.

I'm grieving because I am finally processing all that I pushed away. All that I once couldn't handle or suppressed is coming up at a time I am ready to feel and pour out.

I'm grieving the time I felt was wasted, the prayers I prayed, and the expectations I had. I'm grieving the versions of myself that I had to be to get where I am.

I'm grieving and exhausted because I existed in a way that was silent yet tested all my strength, sanity, and connection to the source.

I'm grieving because I acknowledge what led me to be so selective was being scared. Scared that I couldn't trust people or potentially could be let down by them. Scared to let my guard down. Scared I'd be improperly perceived instead of fully seen, preyed on instead of prayed for, or led to learn yet another life lesson.

I'm grieving the years I didn't process death because its permanent nature was too much to bear, and the love lost was too difficult to conceive.

I'm mourning what was, moving through the emotions, and making a path for my grief to pass. I'm giving myself the support I always needed, the compassion I deserve, and the time and space it takes to heal.

Grief has no time limit—just like love.
You adapt to the void and live again, but that doesn't mean you don't acknowledge the magnitude of the loss. I used to guilt myself for succumbing to waves of grief when they hit.

I would tell myself:
They would want you to be happy.
They would want you to move forward.
They would want you to continue living in a way that makes them proud.

Although those statements may be true, I recognize that the loved ones I lost knew me. They understood my heart, valued my softness, and never invalidated my feelings. They would give me time and compassion if I cried. They wouldn't make me feel bad for feeling my emotions so deeply. If anything, they would wipe tears from my eyes—not judge me for having them.

They not only took up space in my heart...
I know with certainty that I took up space in theirs.

Because I will love them forever, I've made peace with the fact that I may always cry for them, think about them, and crave their advice as I wonder how they would handle certain seasons and situations in life. Not in a way that I no longer live a healthy life, but in a way that honors the truth that their lives impacted mine in the most beautiful, profound, and unforgettable ways.

My grief is not a sign that I can't or don't want to accept reality or move forward. My grief is a sign that I will forever appreciate their impact and existence. I will continue to cherish our memories together. I will always love them.

I am no longer grieving the idea
of what could have or should have been
but finally embracing the power that comes
with accepting what is and what was always meant to be.

It's not okay, but I'm over it.

I'm over replaying it in my mind like a broken record—giving myself a slew of questions pertaining to myself, the world around me, and any aspect of the experiences I referenced in my mind.

I'm over it because whether it was right or wrong, fair or factual, I overcame it. And what you overcome does not need to be opened and reviewed every day.

You take the lesson, apply it, and move forward with your life understanding that you don't have to accept what doesn't align with you or the truth.

There will come a point when you realize this is the very last time.

This is the very last time you are going to surround yourself with people who try with everything in them to dim the light you carry. This is the very last time you're going to hold yourself down, beat yourself up, or convince yourself that you are not capable of or deserve better.

This is the very last time you try to force yourself to feel safe around anyone who was a safe space for someone else to hurt you. This is the very last time you put yourself in a situation your nervous system told you not to entertain. This is the very last time you accept disrespect from those who should have been served distance a long time ago. This is the very last time you beat yourself up over what was done. This is the very last time you will be your own worst enemy.

At this point, accept accountability that you set the stage for your own suffering the entire time.

Because you didn't want to lose people or accept life as is, you allowed yourself to slowly lose yourself, your voice, and your mind.

Sometimes accountability is accepting
that the person you are most upset with is *yourself.*

It is understanding that you must forgive people
when they know not what they do,
and you must forgive yourself for holding on
when God repeatedly told you to let go.

Let the tears that taught you trickle down your face as you open your eyes to the revelation that the hurt in your heart was always valid. Now, it's time to heal.

Now it's time to fully feel everything. Not in a way that drowns you, but in a way that detoxes your mind, body, and soul.

Cry out, scream, and move your body in a way that shakes out all that shook you. Name the emotion holding you hostage, the person or people who hurt you, the experience that traumatized you, and the version of yourself that haunts you.

Articulate and audit the thoughts that torment you and reaffirm to yourself that moving forward comes from letting out all that you kept in.

the healing you hear

SPEAK
IT

Wisdom taught you to be still, but so did stress, people pleasing, and fear. This is the path of your journey that will show you some healing only comes from what you hear.

Perhaps it's time to converse with others and speak the words you couldn't articulate, yet your actions always exposed. Maybe it's time for you to hear your own voice as you look in the mirror and acknowledge you didn't know best then but now you do.

This isn't the time to worry about if someone will receive your message or hide from what needs healing.

This is your season to release your burdens and embrace your peace as you process all things out loud.

Sometimes you simply need to be heard;
not by someone else but by yourself.

Sometimes you simply need to say things out loud so you can
truly grasp how valid your emotions and reactions are or how
needless something is to still think and care about.

Sometimes you need to hear the words in your head spoken and
released from your mind. Sometimes you need to hear yourself
say what you felt and what you experienced so it is concrete and
finally processed.

Here you are—balancing the task of finally processing the past while simultaneously aligning yourself for a better future.

You're somewhere between the middle and the end of the tunnel where the darkness feels familiar, but you can feel the warmth of the light that awaits.

It's a spiritual shift, personal pivot, and transitional season that comes when you're breaking free from old burdens and aligning yourself with new blessings.

Anger was never the enemy.
It was always the secondary emotion,
an indicator that a line was crossed.

It was the evidence that something wrong around me was
rightfully rattling something within me—not because I was
overly sensitive, unable to simply move past it, or merely
because I was lacking the tools or maturity to handle it—but
because it was not okay.

My feelings were always valid, even when I ignorantly viewed
anger as the villain. It was the part of me that cared about my
wellbeing and wanted to protect me most—even when I
understood or wanted to feel it the least.

Perhaps the reason you struggled so long to truly forgive and let certain things go is because you didn't acknowledge that something wasn't right or give yourself room for healthy anger and heavy emotions.

Instead, you pushed your feelings away in hopes of regaining and restoring peace or rushed to empathize and understand why someone hurt you knowingly or unknowingly.

You sought to understand the why behind their actions or inaction more than you allowed yourself to accept what happened or how it truly affected you.

Your pursuit to forgive quickly without allowing yourself to fully feel only delayed your processing and pushed you to resent people in the long run.

I claimed to forgive and thought I did.
In the depth of my body and soul, I knew I didn't.
How could I?

I held on to unforgiveness with both arms, my entire heart, and with every ounce of energy I had.

Even if the offense or its impact didn't leave my mouth, it stayed on my mind weighing on me to the point that reflecting on its memory became a daily occurrence.

That burden drained my spirit and left my nervous system stuck in survival mode. Those memories were played like clockwork; those words echoed on repeat. Neither of those routines ever led to a redo or undo in my life.

It's a web that wears you out.

But how can I call myself free if I can't release what only has the ability to keep me down? How can I be filled and renewed if I can't forgive others or the former versions of myself who hurt me?

Forgiveness is freedom; honesty leads to healing. And truth is… I'm not there yet.

I have faith that one day I will fully forgive you…but I'm not there yet.

Presenting yourself as the emotionally intelligent person who always takes the High Road or the one who forgives quickly without allowing yourself time to feel is sometimes simply self-betrayal and emotional abandonment with a pretty bow on it.

It looks like ignoring your sense of safety for the sake of being accepted. It sounds like never articulating how something impacted you or what you expect out of a relationship because you fear being rejected or misunderstood.

It smells like setting yourself on fire to keep everyone else around you warm while hoping one day they'll extend an ounce of that grace or empathy to you. It feels like hiding your hurt from those around you instead of openly healing your broken pieces because you don't want someone to stab you in the back using information from one of your own shards.

Listen to yourself. Stop trying to excuse or understand the whys of other people more than you heal. Hear the whys within yourself.

Voice your beliefs, boundaries, and needs.
Be your own supporter, advocate, and validator.

You may no longer be viewed as the bigger person to those around you, but you will finally be a safe person within yourself.

Just because you forgave, it doesn't mean you forgot.

Often, what leads you to struggle most and even guilt yourself is looking at situations, friendships, and relationships and saying, "I forgave this person. I forgave myself. Why am I still struggling with this? Why am I still not comfortable? Why do I still not feel safe? Why do I still have shame?"

The truth is you didn't forget.
Your mind and nervous system did not forget.

That doesn't mean you don't love people and forgive them. It also doesn't mean that you don't love or forgive yourself. Healing is a process, so is forgiveness.

You must give yourself compassion through every step.

Next time something triggers you, comes to your mind, or you're in a situation where you realize *I'm dwelling and hurting over something I thought I forgave or let go of*, I encourage you to reframe the situation.

Say you're dealing with a person who hurt you knowingly or unknowingly. Whether this person is someone who brought you pain and acknowledged it with an actual apology, or they are someone who didn't and doesn't care and will likely not ever acknowledge the impact of their actions—ask yourself what did that revelation teach you?

What did you learn about that person and yourself? Did that situation teach you about life, faith, or even psychology?

When you change your view of someone from being an enemy to being someone who instructed you about a life lesson, you realize that they are your teachers. The ways in which you learned should not continue to torment you.

When you're sitting there tempted to self-loathe over something you did or didn't do, said or didn't say—before you are burdened by shame, anger, and regret, ask yourself what that taught you.

Have you learned since then? Have you repented since then? Have you applied your life lessons in a way that not only led you to do better but also become a better person?

You cannot redo anything in the past, but you can allow the lessons you learned from that experience to renew your mind, redirect your focus, and restrengthen your relationship with God.

It would be easier to blame the world for taking our kindness for weakness or saying it's our empathetic, magnetic spirit that attracted narcissistic, manipulative people into our lives. That wouldn't be completely true.

Truth is, many of us are people pleasers who lack boundaries and have a bad habit of excusing toxic behavior from people beyond logic, then considering it our loyalty and love.

Whether we realize it or not, our nurturing, glass half-full and validation-seeking nature often leads us to forget that those around us are people—not projects.

When you look at people and relationships as projects,
you judge their performance or their inability to measure up
as a reflection of your own work, time, and value.

Just because you sacrifice for others
does not mean they will reciprocate
all you've extended.

Some people can't
and others simply lack
the desire to.

The person I was most angry at was myself.

I truly hid myself, silenced myself, and didn't do the right things for myself for reasons that stemmed from fear and rejection. For reasons that developed when I struggled to process and navigate confusion.

So, I settled with not fueling the fire—even though that meant extinguishing my own truth and light.

I let myself down numerous times; yet, viewed it as resilience because I learned to help other people up in the process.

Being unheard taught me to listen and receive without interruption or ego. Being misread taught me to ask questions and view other people's perspective without the presence of bias. Being insecure and anxious taught me to encourage and empathize with others.

Sitting with suppressed pain taught me to sit with others as they stand in and share their truths.

I became a safe space and sanctuary for everyone *but* me.
And that is no one's fault but my own.

Extend compassion and mercy to the part of yourself that pushed away your emotions because you didn't know how or weren't ready to process them.

Speak words of encouragement to the part of yourself that overanalyzed everything and viewed life through the lens of self-doubt—fearful of being rejected or misunderstood.

Create a safe space to release the part of yourself whose delayed processing and discomfort towards anger, disgust, and boundaries led you to suppress everything.

Acknowledge and clap for the part of you that didn't know how to celebrate yourself or your successes but never thought twice to move the goal posts.

Release the hurt version of you through the wisdom, forgiveness, and grace extended from the healed version of you.

Forgive yourself for the storms you created.
Forgive yourself for not asking for help, not seeking wise
counsel, nor implementing a boundary sooner.

Forgive yourself for the times you could have extended more
love, patience, and compassion to someone but instead led with
judgment, apprehension, or pettiness.

Forgive yourself for trying to fix it and only making it worse.
Forgive yourself for trusting the wrong people in your lowest
seasons, which in turn makes it difficult to trust anyone now.

Forgive yourself for being the worst version of yourself.
Forgive yourself for being naïve and foolish.
Forgive yourself for struggling.

Forgive yourself because you did the best you could with what
you knew at the time. Forgive yourself because you deserve
peace, compassion, and mercy.

Forgive yourself for giving it to God, then taking it back.

Forgive yourself because it is time to be free.

Healing the little girl within you
begins with realizing
she never truly left.

You can't take them with you.
You must leave the former versions of yourself behind.

The version of you that is stuck in your mind—the version of
you that was most vulnerable. The version of you that was so
overwhelmed and filled with so many emotions that you
experienced numbness and lost the ability or desire to speak.

The version of you that just wanted to be seen, heard, and
understood. The version of you who needed to be healed,
supported, and loved by the exact type of person you are today.

The past versions didn't know then what you would become.
They did the best they could, learned from each test, and never
gave up.

Their weakness led to your wisdom.
Their struggles led to your strength.

They had to think, react, and be all that they were then, so you
could learn, heal, and become exactly who you are now.

It wasn't your fault. It wasn't for you to fix. You couldn't have known that would happen. You can't keep doing this to yourself.

I know you've convinced yourself that if you wouldn't have done *that*, the outcome wouldn't have been what it was. If you would have said *this*, something else would have happened.

You rack your brain with possible scenarios...
But...
If only I...
I should have...
What if...

You blamed yourself when it seemed no one else would take accountability. You condemned yourself when you realized you couldn't control or correct at all. You suppressed and tried to bury it all when you realized no one was coming to save the day.

But it wasn't your burden to bear,
your cross to carry,
or your sin to suffer for.

That hurt was never yours to hold.

I hear you.

The fragility, vulnerability, and uncertainty in your voice as you articulate all you thought you were past... As you resurrect all the feelings you thought you buried.

You've taken everything out that you've held in—the emotions and experiences you shoved to the top of the closet in your mind. What you wanted to forget and move forward from. So, you tucked them away with the desire to revisit them when you were ready or not at all.

Saying and hearing it outside of your body makes it real.

Although it isn't currently happening, you are reminded of just how much it hurt, changed, and impacted you when it happened.

Just how much it still hurts and impacts you now.

Apologize to the version of yourself that was doing the best they could with what they knew yet carried condemnation and inner criticism.

The version of you that was beyond beautiful yet you badgered yourself into believing you were too much or not enough.

The version of you that needed compassion, reassurance, and love, yet couldn't find it in anyone—not even the person in the mirror.

MORGAN RICHARD OLIVIER

Give yourself grace.

Give yourself compassion, mercy, love, forgiveness, and
understanding—the same amount you are willing to give
everyone around you whether they deserve it or not. Because,
like them, you are doing the best you can and learning in real
time.

Sometimes it takes seasons where it seems like you're taking two
steps forward and 10 steps back for you to truly get it—for you
to truly grasp who you are and what your purpose is.

Be gentle with yourself.

Don't be so unforgiving of the mistakes or the choices you've
made, especially if they worked together to give you the heart
posture, faith, and mindset you have today.

No one is perfect,
and it is time for you to accept
that also includes you.

Pick yourself up and put down all that has been dragging you.

Focus on your own life, mindset, and goals. Free yourself from the need to have validation, support, and understanding from everyone around you.

Healing is an inner job—one that requires accountability, integrity, and an immeasurable amount of compassion.

Yesterday is gone, tomorrow is out of your control, but the present is here waiting for you to join it.

Stop sitting on your potential.
Step into your power and purpose.

There is so much to gain,
but you must lose your desire
to manage, control, and understand it all.

You don't know all the answers,
understand every ordered step,
or clearly see the direction God is leading you—
just know it is best.

Give it to yourself.

The validation, support, and encouragement—give it to yourself.
The love, loyalty, and compassion—give it to yourself.
The closure, apology, and confirmation that it's time to let go—
give it to yourself.

No longer push away your peace because you're waiting for
someone to give you all you gave or would have given them.

Heal for yourself. Learn for yourself.
And all that you need to move forward...
give it to yourself.

You don't realize the weight
you've been carrying
until you put it down.

Peace is often the byproduct of releasing.
Releasing the need to control the outcome.
Releasing fear as you press forward with faith.
Releasing bonds and environments that consistently
steal your joy.

It is only when you make the choice to surrender
that true serenity can flourish in your life.

There is no reward for being the most loyal
person with the least boundaries.

There are only unmet expectations
and painful life lessons.

It seems like everyone loves you when you don't know who you are.

When you don't defend yourself or rock the boat because you fear the reactions or rejection of others more than the impact that suppressing emotions and diluting your truth will bring.

The wrong people will love it when you seek to prove and please them but aligned people will love you and not want you to needlessly punish and invalidate yourself.

Be mindful of the promises you make
to yourself in the midst of your pain.

Pain induced promises to protect yourself
sound awfully similar to curses.

God, cleanse me of any resentment or offense that came from being observant and silent in my seasons of being still and accepting revelation.

Help me forgive others and myself.

Help me release any desire to correct when the whole purpose of the tests and trials were to act as my catalyst. Help me embrace the power of my lessons and the potential impact of the empathy earned through my experiences.

Help me as I let go of burdens that were never intended for me to carry.

MORGAN RICHARD OLIVIER

Praying for those who persecute you and prey on you takes a
level of spiritual maturity that most people are not willing to
experience.

It requires you to silence your flesh and operate fully in your
spirit as you accept that the person in question is a flawed human
being…just like you.

What they did or said may not ever be okay. It may have scarred
you and impacted you in ways that you still can't fully articulate.

No, your prayers may not ever change them,
but they will change you.

Unforgiveness, bitterness, and offense are heavy.
Give yourself time, grace, and support. Then give that person,
situation, and pain to Him.

If I had to teach myself
that your insults, absence,
and opinions do not matter,
then I also taught myself
that your compliments, presence,
and efforts do not hold any weight either.

The conversations you wish you could have with other people, yet discernment tells you it would not be wise, have them with God.

Vulnerably express to Him just how something or someone made you feel. Tell Him all the ways you were impacted and just how much it still affects you now. Confide in Him and let Him know how much an apology or acknowledgement would have meant to you.

If you are the person in need of forgiveness, tell Him how truly sorry you are. Allow the contrition of your heart and sincerity of your sorrow to correct your behavior and mindset.

Tell Him. Rest in the truth that He clearly sees and hears you.

Find the peace and the power to move forward because you fully accept and understand that He knows and understands everything that happened, all you felt, and everything you are currently going through.

He knows what happened to you wasn't right. He knows how much that situation hurt you. He knows just how genuinely sorry you are and all the steps you've taken to fix it and follow His path.

He knows the heart of man and the motives and movements of every person.

Put every emotion, experience, and concern in His hands and keep it there. He is a healer, counselor, and The One who handles all.

You deserve people in your life who will love and respect you both in front of your face and behind your back.

You deserve friendships that allow you to be vulnerable and transparent about your experiences and emotions—without the fear of being invalidated or taken advantage of.

You deserve the compassion and care you so genuinely and graciously give. Make space for those types of relationships in your life and stop tolerating anything less.

Oftentimes, the desire for clarity and conversation is there when your overall objective is to reestablish some form of connection. Whether that is to mend a broken relationship or bring closure to something that has ended.

However, when you have no aspirations of realigning or associating yourself with a person again, that desire is nonexistent.

You begin to desire your peace more than proving your point.

When a former people pleaser gets to the point that they no longer concern themselves with losing people or not being liked, that is when true deliverance and development take place.

When you care more about God knowing the facts of who you are instead of fixating on the feelings of people who think they know who you are—that is how you know you are free.

Much like a person who hasn't eaten for days yet has no appetite when a plate is served, I, too, no longer want it. I no longer crave from you what I learned to cultivate within myself.

That doesn't come from a place of anger. It springs from a space of awareness and acceptance of truth. When I hungered for your support, prayed for your understanding, and thirsted for your love, you not only withheld it from me, but made a spectacle of the fact that I was starving.

You didn't have time, concern, or words to spare when I felt like I was being pulled apart. Suddenly you have compliments, invites, and some feeling of entitlement to my energy now that what was intended to destroy me developed me.

So, no.
You can keep it—all of it.
After all, you are the one who taught me
I didn't need it.

The greatest lesson you've ever gifted me was the truth that I never needed to be aligned with a seat at anyone else's table. I simply needed the faith, competence, and strength to build and stand boldly on my own.

You can be loving and have limits.
You can be kind and not tolerate cruelty.

You can have boundaries. You can say no.
You can opt out of going somewhere because it doesn't sit well
with your spirit or you don't feel safe.

You can remove yourself from the conversation, the
environment, or the friendship...and that doesn't make you a
mean person.

Sometimes doing what's best for you is not going to be
comfortable for you or understood by everyone. However, if you
are growing, healing, learning, and aligning yourself—you will
have to make uncomfortable, difficult, and misunderstood
decisions. That's what it takes to lead you to true healing,
alignment, and growth.

It's easy to worry about what everyone says and thinks and
common to concern yourself about how you're coming off.
But this is the season where you place more importance on
wisdom and alignment than you do acceptance and community.

You cannot love anyone into loving you.
You cannot support anyone into supporting you.
You cannot protect anyone into protecting you.

The sooner you realize that people are the products of their patterns and not your expectations, the sooner you will accept others and yourself as is.

Over time, the voice I didn't use began to echo in my own head.

The happiness that once came from being accepted and included and the comfort I once felt from being isolated and diluted later subsided because I realized that I had to lose myself to gain it.

And for the first time in my life, I was done.

I didn't care how I came across, what anyone said, or if it was perceived as nice. It was time to rebuild parts of myself that I allowed to be broken.

Part of the reason I held grudges against people
was because I never held them accountable.

And that wasn't their fault—that was mine.

Lacking boundaries, extending mercy to malicious intent at the
expense of my mental health, and suppressing my emotions and
experiences added a heaviness to my heart and mind that not
only impacted my identity but also my spiritual growth.

Perhaps the reason many of us hold so much offense and resentment towards others is because we would have wanted to have a healthy conversation with them to bring clarity and forgiveness at the time, but we didn't feel safe to, or we knew it wouldn't be wise to try.

When you reach a point where you can express your truth and testimony in a way that doesn't make you feel emotionally exposed because you have already processed your emotions and found peace—that is when you speak.

When you realize you have nothing to lose yet so much to release, you will have what you once perceived as *difficult conversations* because you are no longer speaking from a place that fears another person's projections or perspective.

You are speaking your truth because you seek to obtain your own peace and power.

You can be uncomfortable.
You can say what needs to be said.
You can change your mind.
You can release and redirect your attention and energy as
needed.

You don't need outside validation.
You don't need to have everything perfect.
You don't need everyone to see or understand you.
You don't need all that you once wanted.

You need to do what God tells you to do,
keep your peace, and live authentically.

Be the person you were created to be.
Be encouraged. Be wise. Be yourself.

You are not responsible for their response.

You are responsible for the tone, words, and amount of vulnerability you choose to express.

You cannot control if the other person understands, believes, or respects what you say.

Your peace is not predicated
by their perception.
Their belief, or the lack of it,
does not tarnish the truths of your life.

Another person's inability to understand or accept the truth that you shared with them is not a reflection of your reality and does not infringe on the validity of anything you've lived.

Even if you feel that person should know better or should have handled your vulnerability in a different way. Even if you expected that person to react differently and wanted them to simply be there for you yet they ended up not supporting or leaving space for your pain at all.

The person you need to focus on is you.

Placing your identity in the invalidation of another human being will cripple your view of self and lead you to question your own voice, if you allow it to.

If your words, pain, and truth are not respected, believed, or properly handled by the person you are confiding then—respect yourself enough to leave that conversation with your peace, confidence, and view of self intact.

Their inability to receive you should never lead to your inability to trust, validate, or love yourself.

You're fighting so hard to explain yourself to those who left you in your lowest season to fight alone.

For some reason, your desire to make them see you simultaneously leads you to lose sight of yourself.

You cover your truth instead of adding it to the conversation because you know you can't trust them with it. Words that would vindicate you go unspoken because you don't want to fall victim to their misinterpretation or intention to disregard you.

You withhold your perspectives as a way of avoiding potential pain.

This doesn't build trust with them. It simply leads you to lose the trust you have within yourself.

Because you have to operate at a minimized level to meet in the middle—you harbor a hidden hurt. One that is perceived by the world as being kindly cordial; yet, serves as a heartbreaking lesson that you can't reconstruct. A closeness with anyone whose presence seemingly constricts you or rids you of your safety.

I placed the level of expectation on you that was never truly fair or fit. I resented you for not reciprocating when you didn't truly realize the extent of what was going on.

The truth is, you acted in a way that aligned with your behavioral patterns. You responded in a way that you always had with everyone else. I just thought it would be different with me...and not in a pity party type of way. I thought my place in your life meant something.

It hurt me because if the tables were turned, those actions and behaviors you exhibited wouldn't have been mine.

But that's life.

Sometimes there is no reciprocation, clarity, or justice. Sometimes you just leave the cards where they fall and leave with the lesson that your life, sanity, and alignment are not some game.

You gain understanding and maturity from that experience and lose the offense and immaturity that led you to them.

Where there is projection, there is invalidation.

No matter how honest you are, how deep your truth may be, or
how logical your words may seem—if the person you're
expressing yourself to is only capable of receiving from a lower
level of awareness or is projecting their own lens unto you, you
will feel misunderstood. You will feel unseen.

And if repeatedly experienced over time, you will feel unsafe.

You will learn the hard way that in those moments of
vulnerability, it's never about them truly hearing you or holding
space for you.

They're not receiving your message.
They're only reflecting themselves.

You let them be wrong.
You let them treat you how they wanted to treat you.
You let them say what they wanted to say.
And this time, you need to let them learn.

Let them learn that though life isn't fair, neither is favor.

Let them learn that though you can come against people, talk
about people, hurt people, and steal from people—you cannot
stop the purpose on someone's life, the anointing they have, or
the gifts they possess.

All you can do is stop that connection you had with them.

If they sat back and watched you suffer,
let them stand back and watch you thrive.

A strong opinion is not a fact.
A loud, confidently spoken projection is not a fact.
Misinformation that goes uncorrected is not a fact.

If someone cannot grasp the simple truth of this statement, then
why are you so persistent on proving yourself or proving
something to them?

They aren't looking for clarity.
They are looking to confirm whatever bias they have.

Remember this before you allow the projections and opinions of
others to impact your inner voice or view of self.

You know you.

You know your intentions, the details of your experiences, and
the depth of your emotions. Most importantly, God knows.

Don't ever let the feelings of others
distort the facts of who you are.

My identity is not a reflection of your opinion
yet for so long your acceptance, understanding,
and validation was my idol.

It lifted me up and tore me down.

My desire to be seen, loved, and respected by you only revealed
how badly I needed to see, love, and respect myself.

God, help me soften the parts of my heart hardened by hurt.

Help me to respond to people and situations with love and mercy—when my nervous system wants to react with freezing or frustration.

I can't fully live for you if every move I make is set on my own terms. Show me who you want me to be and guide me in every ordered step and ordered stop I must take to get there.

You are the common denominator in every aspect of your life.

Sometimes, you are the problem. Sometimes it's your inability to identify and accept an issue within yourself that is leading you to align with people and opportunities that do not align with your overall good.

You can be healing, praying, and hoping with the best intentions yet still be out of order, spiritually immature, and in need of a reality check.

Hold yourself accountable and address all that is within you. You are a work in progress, and there is no shame in seeking correction.

Make sure that unconditional love you have for family or friends is not a soul tie. Fast, pray, and seek wise counsel. Make an effort to understand your dreams. Respect your discernment and pay attention to how your body reacts to certain energies and environments. Some bonds are not meant to stay or be restored.

You prayed for revelation and God provided it. Now ask yourself why you refuse to let go when it only hurts you to hold on.

Accept when what you perceive as loyalty and desire for community is actually spiritual disobedience that leads to disorder.

The tie that kept our souls connected was built on memories, emotions, and unforgiveness.

It was a knot that dragged and depressed me through time but one that still left me believing with the right time, exposure, and conditions...things could get better.

It was a tie that left me interceding and empathetic towards you but stole sleep and serenity from me. It left me quick to speak life over you, yet never interject when you spoke death over me.

My ego saw myself as a helper; your spirit saw me as a host.

Although my inability to identify and articulate that truth cost me my peace, it also shifted my perspective and led me to lean on my faith in a season where I was releasing my feelings.

I was forced to focus on having a healthy, aligned future—not simply return to what was familiar.

It was disarming the distraction of desire. The desire to restore. The desire to fix. The desire to have God repair something in my life that He removed because He knew its presence could only hurt me.

I've spent years trying to convince God to restore, reconcile, and reveal things to a world He didn't even want me to be a part of.

And now, after all this time, I'm grateful He didn't give me all that I once prayed and asked for.

He loved me too much then,
and I love myself too much now.

God never told you that.

He never said He would restore it. Maybe that's what you wanted, but that doesn't mean it's what you need.

He never told you that your plan perfectly aligns with the plan He has for you, that the friendship or family bond that broke your heart is one He wants to revive, or that the person you invested time in is the one He has called and is preparing to be in your life.

Don't confuse your efforts, prayers, and desires with His will, ways, or hopes for you.

It's amazing how hard we will fight to leave a space open in our hearts, lives, and minds for those who do not belong there. How long we are willing to wait for people to see us, love us, and understand us before we accept the fact that they are not meant for us.

How long we will ignore or misconstrue the signs and revelations God uses to instruct us to let go of something because we want or hold on to hope.

That unwillingness to release is not faith—it is foolishness.

At some point you must tell yourself that you do not want anything God doesn't want for you and that it's better to be disappointed than destroyed.

If you know God is able to do all things but He doesn't want to do something for you, rest assured you shouldn't want it either.

I prayed and fasted for revelation then cried and struggled to accept it once it was received.

And that's because opening my eyes was one thing but closing the door to what was revealed within me and who was revealed around me was another.

My heart did not want to comprehend what God so clearly communicated.

To say you are blessed with spiritual vision yet choose to be blind to everything God has revealed to you is not only foolish, it's also disobedient.

God clearly showed you and confirmed to you in a way that couldn't be ignored. Quit acting like He isn't answering because you don't want to heed the warning.

Release what you wanted so you can align with what you need.

After you're all out of excuses and exhausted from the amount of pain you tolerated for the sake of love, friendship, family, or optics, you will understand that sometimes the wisest action to take is to simply let go.

You can love others yet have enough love for yourself to stop rebuilding bonds that will only continue to break you.

Pray and press on with the acceptance that turning the page is pivotal for protecting your peace and purpose.

Your freedom, closure, peace, and joy will not be found in the words of people whose words destroyed you.

It will not be found by gaining access or presence to people who left you at your most vulnerable and broken times.

It's not about restoring or rekindling for all of us. Many of our breakthroughs are on the other side of releasing. Releasing offense, anger, resentment, regret, condemnation, the idea of how it should have been, the idea of what you should have said, the idea of the justice or fairness or clarity that you wanted.

My desire to ever converse or be in close proximity to you is
nonexistent.

Not because I have hate in my heart, unforgiveness in my soul,
or grudge has me by its grip. It's because I have nothing for you
and want absolutely nothing from you.

I see you clearly. I see myself clearly.
I've learned what I needed to learn.

When you were loud, I silently observed.
When you boldly and consistently served disrespect,
I served distance and didn't take the bait of distraction.

I didn't fight back because it wasn't my battle nor was any of it
worth fighting for.

If that's a win for you—keep it.
And I will keep my peace, lessons,
and pruned life as the prize it is.

Let them off the hook.

On the other side of *letting them* you will also have to process all that you felt. Genuinely release them so you can no longer have to feel it.

You're going to have to let them off the hook because holding on and harboring unforgiveness is what's keeping you anchored to the past and drowning in your emotions.

I've been the person who someone had to forgive.
I've been the person who hurt others knowingly and
unknowingly.

I've been the person who had to seek help and fully depend on
God.

I say this because it reminds me of the importance of forgiving
others while also accepting that it's a person's choice to take
accountability for their life, healing, and development.

You don't ever have to go out of your way to speak to them again. You don't ever have to go out of your way to see them again. You don't ever have to go out of your way to prove you let something go by letting someone back in your life.

The notion that resilience and forgiveness are shown by allowing someone reentry into your life or space is not a testament to your healing, maturity, or strength.

Sometimes it's proof that you'd rather validation and people pleasing more than protecting your peace and walking in wisdom.

No one has tempted me to harden my heart
more than people I had a soft spot in my heart for.

No one has hurt me more
than people I've tried to help.

I love you—that was never in question. The question that remains is if loving you is enough to put myself in the position to be hurt again. Hurt in a way that made me question my sanity, my ability to trust others, and my ability to trust myself.

Everything within me wishes I could view you as I once did, feel like peace around you, or let my guard down...but I can't.

And I want to so badly.

My nervous system and discernment fight me.

I've cried rivers about it, prayed earnestly for it, and fasted more times than I can count. I've tried to see it from multiple perspectives, held myself accountable, inserted a slew of whys to excuse your behavior, and even silenced my own wisdom in hopes that healthy restoration is possible.

But the most painful revelation I've received and accepted is the truth that I don't feel safe with you. That's not because I'm refusing to let something go or as a result of my own pride but because I shouldn't.

I don't feel safe because I'm not.

I learned that you cannot lose anyone who is not with you.

Sometimes that is very difficult to accept—especially if people
are always in your face, in your group photos, or trying to be in
your life. Just because someone is in your circle, does not mean
they are in your corner.

Just because someone is constantly calling to check on you,
wanting to know your next steps, or asking you questions,
doesn't mean they're engaged, interested, or truly in it for you for
the right reasons.

Instead of being angry when people reject you, abandon you,
gossip about you, or are not there for you to the capacity that
you've been there for them or would be for them—look at it as
an answered prayer.

Look at it as revelation of who they are
and where they deserve to be in your life
but *never* a reflection of your worth.

You taught me.

And even if those lessons were learned the hardest, most frustrating way—the pain had a greater purpose. The pressure refined me, and all the unspoken darkness led to an undeniable light.

You taught me that the ugliest intentions of one can yield the most beautiful insights in another. And I say this not to put you down but to lift the truth that God will truly use what was intended to hurt you for your good.

God used you to redirect me, to teach me, and to show me that I was not yet prepared or aligned to be the person He created me to be.

So instead of looking at you as rotten, I should thank you for taking me through the test that ultimately watered my spiritual fruits.

MORGAN RICHARD OLIVIER

Release what has released you.

Release that person who already released you.
Release that job that already released you.
Release the expectation, timeline, and the life plan you had for
yourself that has already released you.
Release the desire to revive, rekindle, or retrieve what has
already released you.

I understand it's painful. I understand you put years into that
friendship or relationship, just hoping that person would change
or become the version of themselves you know they have the
potential to be.

I know you're hard on yourself and imagined being in a different
place in life by now. But in all these areas, I need you to
understand that acceptance is critical and alignment is key.

You can grieve what you lost, mourn what never came to pass,
and still have enough love, respect, and spiritual maturity within
yourself to loosen your grip on something God does not want for
you.

The longer you try to force something or someone that is not
meant to continue on your journey, the more you hold yourself
back from all the blessings, people, and inner growth that are
meant for you.

the healing you hear

There will come a time when those
who mistreated you will miss you.

When you are tempted to rekindle relationships
that God not only revealed but ordered you to release,
I pray you are directed by discernment and don't mismanage the
wisdom you've acquired.

God, I remove every burden from my head and place it at your feet—walking away knowing that surrendering it into your hands is what will truly heal my heart and detox my mind.

I'm not holding anything against you.
I'm simply no longer holding space for you.

The home you once had in me is still standing,
but you are no longer welcome to stay.

The person I am—the one who loved without bounds, supported
without needing to be asked, and showed you that true bonds are
safe outlets to confide in—never left, but my desire to be a part
of your life has.

My energy, awareness, and essence are still overflowing.
It is your access that is denied.

God is not restoring you simply to bring you back to your familiar or comfortable state.

He is restoring and repositioning you to reach mental, spiritual, and emotional levels you have yet to experience.

Some restoration within you can only begin after you release what and who is around you.

You must accept that you can't redo or rewrite a single page of your life story, but you can reframe and renew your mind in a way that helps you pivot.

Yes, your feelings and emotions are valid, but you must make the choice to process what you've suppressed and release what restricts you from living in peace.

Yes, *that* happened but life didn't end there.

Yes, you should have known or done better then. Now, you have the tools and lessons only that situation or season could teach you.

Yes, you lost yourself in that season, but from your lowest point you found God, healing, and a new perspective.

Sometimes we get so wrapped up in replaying the pain in life we overlook the power that came from it. We fixate and get frustrated because God allowed something to happen, yet we conveniently ignore all the favor, strength, and grace He extended and the ways He made to overcome it.

We are not meant to live in our thoughts.
We are meant to live fully in the present.

Into the depths of the river my tears once cried,
I threw away the keys that unlock any desire
to revive the toxic patterns I had
or anyone and anything that benefited from them.

If you want peace, take it off the pedestal.
No matter what *it* is.

Whether it is the plan for your life, the love and support of others, or simply your desire to know the next step. The more you try to force and fixate on what is not in your control, the more you will block the flow of what truly is sent in alignment for you.

Let it be.

Surrender it to God, fix your focus, and honestly identify when you have turned an aspiration into an idol.

Accept the outcome.
Acknowledge what is over.
Surrender and let it flow.

Resisting all that has been revealed within you and around you will only render you distracted.

Respect your wins and wounds, suffering and success, pain and passion. Release all that God confirmed no longer serves you. Renew your mindset. Realign yourself.

Find peace in the fact that all things are working together. Not just the positive aspects, even in negative experiences there is a necessary exposure. In every loss, there is an undoubtable lesson.

No amount of dwelling can undo what is done, and all the crippling anxiety of what's to come still cannot control it.

So, let it be as you become.

Become wiser with every step forward in the journey you take. Become more empathetic, understanding that although external factors may be different, the emotions each person feels are variations of the same. Become unstoppable as you recognize and embrace the undeniable strength and spiritual authority within you.

Become at peace with the person you truly are,
and protect the life you were created to live.

And this is the part of the journey where you leave it behind.

You leave behind the desire to fix what you didn't break.
You leave behind memories of injustice and errors as you truly appreciate the insight and understanding it brought.
You leave behind the imposter syndrome and fear of being viewed as imperfect or unable.
You leave behind what could have been or should have been as you simply accept what is.

This is the part where you acknowledge that what you once viewed as rejection was truly revelation needed for your alignment. It's time to give more energy and attention to the present and stop being hindered and hurt by the past.

The world keeps turning,
and now it's time to turn the page.

When you can't find the words, pray.
When you can't bear to stand, kneel.
When you can't forget, reframe.

When you are ready to heal, let go.
When you are ready to take your power back…
speak.

Sometimes it takes enduring peaks and valleys,
experiencing the joys and pains of trial and error,
and sitting with suffering and success in seasons
of accountability, assessment, and authenticity
to truly understand the power of your words,
truth, and energy.

Words have always held great meaning to me. My love language is words of affirmation, and I have the gift of speaking and writing. Of course, I value words.

However, as I began to grow, heal, and embrace my purpose—I had to learn that not everyone's words *or lack of words* should carry the same amount of weight and impact.

No human's words—including my own—should be meditated on, respected, and repeated more than God's words.

Distraction is easy to fall into when you lack discernment which is why you must be wise and focused when it comes to allocating your energy. Not every thought of your own or attack by someone else is worthy of your entertainment. Not every word warrants a response.

Audit and edit your thoughts. Pray more than you ruminate. Accept that embracing your authenticity will cause you to fall out of alignment with people you always wanted to be accepted by—including friends and family.

Understand that not everyone will love, protect, and support you. Realize that no lie said to you or about you can erase who you are and what you've experienced. Seek truth, peace, and healing over your mind and life.

The world will always throw words at you. The words you give your time, energy, and attention to will impact and influence you most.

the healing you hear

LIVE
IT

Be seen,
take up space,
and use your voice.

Operate out of discernment,
no matter how difficult that may be,
and make the best choices
for your overall well-being.

It's not about comfort and acceptance.
It is about completion and alignment.

God, I just want to see myself how you see me and speak to myself in a way that reflects your scriptures and words.

When doubt begins to flood my mind, I want your words to come to my memory and flow from my lips.

Remaining steadfast and secure in who I am and to whom I belong.

When was the last time you truly saw yourself?

No, not the version you spruce up to show the world or the picture-perfect person everyone interacts with on social media. I'm talking about your true and imperfect yet authentic self.

No matter how long it has been, look again.

Peel back those expectations and insecurities. Embrace the beautiful soul who is stoically standing underneath it all. Shine your light without the concern of making others uncomfortable. Validate yourself as you recognize just how amazing you are.

Walk with intention and wholeheartedly expect the life you are praying and preparing for. No matter how odd it may feel and even if your voice shakes, speak life over yourself. Use discernment as you begin to share unspoken testimonies.

Discover the peace that comes when you detox your mind, body, and spirit—giving yourself permission to release and reset. Prioritize yourself.

Build your relationship with God, focus on your wellness, heal what hurts, say no when needed, celebrate your strengths, and love all that you are.

This is not the season you search the world with endless questions. This is the season you search yourself and respect the fact that most of your answers are already within you.

You are beautiful. You are worthy.
You are amazing just the way you are.

Do not let the world or your own insecurities lead you to
question all that you are. You are more than enough and more
powerful than you know.

We live in a world that is so diluted with filters, feature altering
apps, and body goals we forget that our bodies are not meant to
be perfectly symmetrical or unblemished. We are not dolls or
animated characters. We are human.

We have scars, cellulite, stretch marks, and loose skin. We have
varicose veins, sunspots, and pores. That doesn't make us less
beautiful. That is merely proof we have lived.

It's your heart, mindset, and soul that radiate the most beauty.
Tend to that. Build your character, shape your focus, and lose the
weight of unattainable expectations.

You—no matter your weight, height, color, or bone structure —
are beautifully, wonderfully, and purposefully made. Embrace
that truth and yourself fully.

Stand on your worth.

You already have what it takes.

You already have the character, qualities, and experience needed to thrive in that place you're praying to be. You simply need to walk out of your comfort zone and walk boldly into your purpose.

The wait is over.
The only person who can hold you back now is you.

Oh, how beautiful you are.

How your aura radiates when you step into a room. Your kind spirit brings serenity and strength to every person you speak to.

I pray you embrace your authenticity and realize the impact of the light you so genuinely emit.

Don't ever let this bitter world rob you of your sweetness.

You are love.
You are loved.

the healing you hear

You don't have to drown yourself to keep anyone else afloat.

You don't have to hide what you've built to make anyone feel secure. You don't have to guilt yourself for growing and outgrowing through life. It is not your responsibility to be properly seen by everyone, nor is it your responsibility to make anyone see the potential, flaw, or truth within themselves.

Let it be and let yourself go for once.

Let go of the idea that you have to be the strong one to the point of exhaustion. Let go of the belief that you must always be without boundaries to be viewed as loyal.

Let yourself be great.
Let yourself be fulfilled.
Let yourself be challenged outside of your comfort zone.
Let yourself discover and dive into the unknown.

Let yourself simply be. And be at peace with that.

Some question your spiritual gifts, wisdom, and ability to see their motives because you don't acknowledge all that you're aware of.

Because you don't match energy.
Because you are kind to those who treated you
poorly to your face and behind your back.
Because you still love and rise in situations they would have handled with hatred and destruction.

Those people are not your problem. They are your reminder of how important personal developments and a relationship with God are.

There will be people who call you fake because the fruit of your life doesn't match the fiction they chose to believe, spread, or project upon you.

There will be people who believe in the goodness of God and the power of inner work because you walk in wisdom and truth.

You are the one who dictates which group influences and inspires you.

Yes, you're strong but you still need support.
Yes, you're dependable, but you still need someone you can
trust. Yes, you're understanding, but you need to also be
comprehended.

Burnout yields no badge.
Reciprocation is the recipe for healthy relationships.

Not allowing those around you to support you, check on you,
and love you in the ways that you need will only hurt you and
your relationships in the end.

I understand that this is not intentional. You show love with your
presence, words, and time. But remember that balanced, healthy
bonds require you to allow others the space and safety to learn
how to love and lead you.

There will come a time when you need a listening ear, a helping
hand to get you from one version of yourself to the next, and a
safe place to land.

Give your loved ones the ability and understanding of how to
learn and love you in the ways you need them to.

Doing so doesn't make you a burden to them.
It makes them balanced with you.

What you have cannot be destroyed or duplicated.

Your authenticity, energy, and impact are all strengths
within you that cannot be touched, tainted, or torn from you.

All the world can try to do is convince you not to show up
as who and all you truly are.

One of your greatest powers
is reflected in your ability
to transmute energy—
not your willingness to match it.

A creative does not have enemies,
we have inspiration.

We turn our pain into poetry.
We turn your lies into literature.
We turn ambiguity into art.

We do not conform to the world
because we know our purpose and gifts
are meant to transform it.

Pray more than you vent.
Ask more than you assume.

The world is full of
deception and doubt.

Calling it how you see it
is often the recipe
for being loud and wrong.

The reason God didn't clear it up, fix those broken pieces, or fully vindicate you is because you have an *in spite of* testimony.

A testimony that shows those assigned to your life that even if things didn't unfold the way you wanted in the natural realm, it still speaks volumes about God's strength and the impact of living a spiritually led life.

Sometimes your testimony doesn't look like a fairy tale or fairness because it is intended to reveal the true power of faith and favor.

MORGAN RICHARD OLIVIER

When the cross you carry doesn't feel like yours to hold, it's tempting to be angry at the world and allow your heart to turn cold.

It's heavy and hurting, all that you must go through. You wonder who the world actually sees—the cross or you.

As time passes and your ego subsides, you realize there's a greater purpose for the thorn in your side.

The fruits of the spirit stand stoically behind when you release the weights of anger and the battle in your mind.

By embracing the empathy, endurance, and understanding of all God can do, you realize carrying the cross is needed for you to become the most impactful version of you.

In a world that tries to label you every chance it gets, I need you to remember that only you have the power to choose what you receive and respond to.

Struggles and mistakes do not define you. The family you were born into and the area you grew up in does not define you. Rumors and gossip do not define you. Diagnosis and disabilities do not define you. Personal insecurities and opinions of ignorant people do not define you. Your measurements and weight do not define you.

Remember who you are, all you've overcome, and all that you're preparing for.

Silence the noise, nonsense, and negative self-talk as you respect the journey you've had, the lessons you've learned, and the resilient person you've become.

Keep going, keep growing, and keep glowing.
You know who you are and who you are called you to be.
And *that* is your superpower.

As you give yourself permission to grow and heal, something amazing happens. You discover yourself.

Much like unwrapping a gift, as you begin to peel back the roots of pain, expectation, and false beliefs, the view of your authentic self blooms.

The journey of self-love and discovery is not always comfortable or understood, but it is a path that will lead you to development, purpose, and peace.

It requires honesty, vulnerability, and the courage to face parts of yourself you may have been avoiding. But it is worth it.

As you heal, pay attention to what lights you up. What brings you peace? What values do you hold that are unshakable? What dreams have you tucked away that are longing to be realized?

Do not be afraid to evolve. Embrace your growth, celebrate your resilience, and allow yourself to change. You're not just healing—you're blooming.

You're becoming more comfortable and confident as each day passes. The world needs exactly who you are.

Continue to explore, grow, and become.
The journey of learning and loving oneself
is the most important journey you'll ever take.

I don't need to know what you think, say, or believe when I stand on what I know.

I know my name. I know who I am. I know why I'm here.

I don't need to entertain your opinion of me.
I don't need your compliments or criticisms to narrate my innermost thoughts. I don't need to prove my place or purpose to you.

My power does not come from your approval, and my value is not determined by your views.

I am capable, competent, and strong enough to be exactly who I was created to be.

You had to go through it
to get to your gift.

Thank God for allowing the fire
to refine you and not consume you.

For showing you mercy when you were most foolish and
compassion when you lost your way. If it were not for His
goodness and grace, you wouldn't be standing here today.

So, release the cycle of grunting over the past and be grateful for
the greater purpose and lessons that sprang forth. God kept you
for a reason. Give Him glory and keep going.

I'm grateful.
For every life experience and every lesson it left behind.
For every tear that crossed my face and every season that opened my eyes.

I'm grateful because every pain shifted my perspective, every 'no' aligned me with a greater 'yes,' and every ending positioned me with an even greater beginning.

I'm grateful for the lessons, faith, and awareness that grew from it all. Everything the enemy intended for harm, God used for good. Accepting that truth is a blessing that outweighs the burdens I've carried for too long.

Be proud of yourself.

You know more than anyone else all that you endured and experienced. You silently fought battles alone, all while boldly being there to love and support those around you.

There were times you felt you were losing your comfort, sanity, and self in every step forward; but, you continued the healing journey and allowed your own plan for your life to stay behind.

Though it took every ounce of faith, focus, and strength you had within you, you never gave up.

And that is beautiful, powerful, and something to be proud of.

You made it.

You overcame every obstacle that was intended to hold you back. You developed from each detour that was sent to destroy you. You learned from every loss and gained a greater appreciation of grace along the way.

The mountain that once clouded your mind and stood in your way is the vantage point you now teach and speak from.

You are worthy of every good thing coming for you.

You are capable of achieving far more than what's available to you in your comfort zone. You are deserving of every opportunity, promotion, and source of abundance you worked for. You are ready to level up and embrace every ounce of joy life has to give.

God is doing a new thing within you and with all that is concerning you. You deserve peace, happiness, and inner freedom.

It is yours to have, you simply must make the choice and give yourself permission to fully embrace it.

MORGAN RICHARD OLIVIER

And after years of creating,
she came to the realization that
she was, in fact, the art.

Listen to and make time for yourself.
Take up space and use your voice.
Challenge your comfort more than
you question your capabilities.
Dream and conquer your fears.

Forgive and learn from the person you once were.
Be the person you were created to be.

Come out of your hiding place.
You must stop selling yourself short and playing it safe.

There is a reason you experienced all you went through, but with exposure comes the realization that this life requires more of you. A version of you that is wise, strong, and knows how to react. A version of you that always keeps your self-control and character intact.

You have been refined for such a time as this.
The world is waiting.

I spent years picking apart every part of myself.
Criticizing and critiquing the imperfections of my body so much
that I didn't appreciate its beauty.

Only to look back and realize just how beautiful I was…just how
powerful my presence was…just how needed my empathy was.

I people pleased, masked my emotions, and minimized myself
only to later realize that I was good enough, strong enough, and
worthy enough just the way I was.

To the version of myself that found it easier to put myself down
and feared lifting myself up, I forgive you. Now, we have to part
ways.

The person I am called to be is meant to speak life and I can only
do that if I genuinely, honestly, and lovingly start with me.

What do you believe about yourself?

Not what everyone says or how you feel they see you.
Not who you're expected to be or the titles you've lived
throughout your life.

But who are you underneath it all?

You're an amazing listener because you know what it's like to go unheard. You are a powerful encourager because you know what it's like to suffer and succeed with minimal support. You're a valuable safe space for others because you know what it's like to walk with the weight of the world on your shoulders and place your trust in the wrong people.

Your greatest darkness aligned you with the purest light and your ugliest wounds equipped you with beautiful wisdom.

God wasted nothing,
and that is why you can clearly see
His hand in everything.

Sometimes healing the former version of yourself comes in the form of becoming the type of person they would feel safe coming to and confiding in.

The person you longed for was *you* all along.

The type of person who listens without judgment, gives without motive, and loves without bounds.

The one whose presence brings peace and whose hugs bring hope. The person whose compassion reminds the world that there are still people who care and whose eyes carry a light that can lead even a stranger out of darkness.

You did more than pray for the change you wanted to see in the world.

You became it.

Create safe spaces for people—especially those you consider your family and friends.

Do not assume without asking.
Do not talk about people when you can easily talk to them.
Do not invalidate the experiences and emotions of others just because you don't understand or haven't encountered them yourself.

You have no idea the battles people fight or thoughts they must encounter each day.

Don't let the tormenting voice in their head be yours.

God has a point to prove with you.

Someone somewhere is holding on to your memory as proof that there are still good people out there.

Someone somewhere is replaying your words of hope and inspiration as they try to combat their negative thoughts and the insecurities that swirl around in their mind.

Someone somewhere remembers your smile and the twinkle in your eye as you showed them sincere kindness and compassion.

Someone somewhere thinks of your persistence and every word of encouragement you spoke that aligned with your actions when they are tempted to give up or procrastinate.

Maybe you think you are just another person in this world, but to someone out there your presence, voice, and genuine nature means the world to them.

Thank you for being my person.

A person who I can truly, vulnerably, and honestly confide in
without fear of judgment or potential of mistrust. Thank you for
being my shoulder to cry on, helping hand when I need it, and
open arms that exude safety and support.

There were times in my life where I lost all sense of direction.
You latched on to me in my darkest moments and were a guiding
light that led me back to who I was and where I needed to be.
You were safe eyes to look into and trust; a constant reminder to
heal and never look back.

With a loving tone and genuine advice, your voice in my head
was sometimes the only thing that got me through the day.

To say that I'm grateful is an understatement.
Saying that I love you is a given.

Thank you for being who you are
and loving me as I am.

To be fully seen,
to be fully heard,
to be fully known,
to be fully protected,

is to be fully loved.

You do not have to become an advocate for all that affected you.

You do not have to share your testimony with the world around you simply because they inquire or expect it, if you know it will shatter the world within you.

Your experiences, traumas, and lessons are yours.

You dictate if you keep them for yourself or open up to those who have proven worthy of receiving them.

Normalize giving people time and space to share their story when they are ready. You are not obligated or entitled to anyone's information, vulnerability, or testimony—no matter how close you are to them or who they are to you.

A major component of creating a safe space is knowing your place.

Sometimes you will be an open book that no one makes an effort to read. Sometimes you'll have so much to say, and no one will ever ask for it.

And in the times you feel unheard, misunderstood, or completely invalidated—remember that you are the only person who fully and truly knows you.

Your truth is not diminished simply because it is not known. Your value does not decrease simply because someone else does not recognize it.

Love and validate yourself.

Everyone else is just *lagniappe*.

You deserve a peaceful life.
A life filled with joy, safety, and authenticity.
You deserve a life where you wake up in the morning excited to live. A life that challenges, inspires, and waters you.

You deserve every single good thing that life has to offer you.

You are ready to fully immerse yourself into a life of peace and purpose at a level you have yet to experience. You are ready to step into the seasons you've been pruning, praying, and preparing for.

With beauty, intelligence, and confidence that shakes the very ground she walks on—she is a disruptor.

Strong, strategic, and equipped with spiritual insight that shatters glass ceilings and builds bridges for others to flourish—she is empowered.

She is a force to be reckoned with, a natural nurturer, and a shining light to everyone who crosses her path.

She is powerful.
She is authentic.
She is unforgettable.

She is *you.*

Please don't spend your life, youth, beauty, and talent on people pleasing. Don't silence yourself trying to keep the peace with everyone but yourself.

See, love, and respect who you are—even if no one else does. Even if no one else appreciates you, supports, protects, or sees the value of all that you are... You must do that for yourself.

You have your whole life ahead of you.

Don't spend your time trying to be everything to everyone and have no fulfillment within yourself. Don't get so wrapped up in your pain that you lose the ability to embrace joy. Don't get so wrapped up in titles that you do not get to discover and learn the uniqueness that is you.

Know that you're not alone on this journey. And even though it is filled with peaks and valleys, highs and lows, it is also filled with great meaning.

Learn to tune out the noise of your inner critic and let the projections of others fall off your back. There will be people who get it, and you will figure it out. The people who want to see you win will clap for you even when you can't clap for yourself.

Don't give up. Believe in yourself. Keep God at the center of everything you do and always work on the things no one can take from you.

You have a purpose. Now you must discover what that is so you can walk boldly in it.

You aren't meant to fit in, be seen, and be understood by everyone. And that is the beauty of letting go of insecurity, expectations, and the desire to be accepted.

You become aligned.

You attract the type of person you are and the type of person you want to be. There's no begging, forcing, or trying to make space for you.

It is there waiting, ready, and completely yours.

There are people waiting for you to arrive as your authentic self.

People waiting for you to share your testimony, shine your light, use your voice, and show up as the person you've been purposed to be.

There are women who need to hear your stories, look into your eyes, feel the warmth of your hugs, and understand that they are not alone. There are men who need to know that their emotions and experiences matter—that you care, that you're here to listen, and that you're a safe space.

You not only need you, but your family line needs you. So does the world.

That will require you to be uncomfortable. That will require you to be mistreated, misunderstood, and openly rejected. With that requirement and responsibility comes the power—the truth that many people need to hear.

You need to be all that you are so others can see just how possible it is for them to do the same.

Take off insecurity—it no longer fits you.
Put on your confidence and shine like never before.

Zip up the dress, let your hair down, look in the mirror,
and soak in the sight of all that is you.

From the spiritual crown on your head to the high heels on your
feet, you embody what you once envisioned. You are poised,
living in peace, and beaming with joy.

The woman you've been healing, pruning, and preparing for is
no longer a desire.

You're looking at her.

With that vision comes provision.

God already prepared a place for you
and an opportunity to meet and connect
with everyone aligned with your purpose.

They are there. You are ready.

You just must release what you had
to fully receive what is waiting for you.

People are going out of their way to bless you, speak highly of you, and appreciate the essence of who you are.

People are praying for you, encouraging you from afar, and loving you both in front of your face and behind your back.

There comes a point when you must stop expecting to be mistreated, misunderstood, or mishandled because that is what you've experienced before. Not everyone is the person or people who hurt you.

Embrace and appreciate the aligned, healthy, and loving relationships you now have. Be open to receive all the amazing bonds to come.

It was always within you.

Everything you try to encourage out of others, find within the world, and prepare yourself for. It was always there.

You simply needed to sit with, heal for, and discover the person within you.

The words tied to releasing your pains, soothing your soul, and developing the greatest version of you were always meant to come from your mouth and be heard in your own voice.

You need it to heal, honor, and hold space for you.

One day, when I breathe my last breath, I want to leave the world behind knowing that my purpose was fulfilled. Truly grateful for the journey I lived and fully confident of where I'm going.

Knowing that my words had meaning, my efforts impacted people in a positive way, and the love within me was truly felt and spread around me.

I want to know that it all meant something—my experiences, gifts, and mindset. I want to know that my words will whisper in someone's mind whenever they need encouragement, empowerment, or even the slightest ounce of empathy.

I want to know that my journey led me to cross paths with people and leave them better than I found them.

Nothing I acquire in this life can go with me,
but there's peace in knowing how much I can leave behind.

Love who you are,
as you embrace the journey
that shaped you.

You're a fraction of who you once were
yet more whole than you've ever been.

You're at peace, in control, and content.

There is wisdom in your words, empathy that shines in your
eyes, and an undeniable strength in your stance.

The tone of your thoughts are just as compassionate as the
conversations you cultivate.

You're resilient, dynamic, and bold because you withstood and
grew from your most difficult, weakest, and silent seasons.
You've reached heights but never forgot where you came from.

You know, trust, and protect yourself in a way that not only
supports who you are now, but also soothes the former version of
you who needed your own love, reassurance, and care.

MORGAN RICHARD OLIVIER

Acknowledgments

To the person who has welcomed my words,
I thank you for not only embracing my journey
but also embarking on your own.

I thank you for meeting my experiences with empathy
and accepting my lessons with love.

May you never forget that healing, happiness, and wholeness
are not found by running to the outside world.
They are developed by returning to the stillness within
your most authentic self.

About the Author

Morgan Richard Olivier is an American best-selling author, advocate, and speaker. With a passion for writing that serves as a form of therapy for both herself and her audience—Morgan's outlet for expression fosters and supports conversations that are needed to stop stigmas and support healing, self-acceptance, and personal growth.

Since publishing her first book *Questions, Christ, and the Quarter-Life Crisis* in 2020, she has gone to publish four best-selling poetry and prose collections: *Blooming Bare* (2021), *The Tears That Taught Me* (2022), *One Still Whisper* and also *The Strength That Stays* both in 2023, and *The Freedom of Forward* in 2024.

Morgan has become a source of encouragement and empowerment to both men and women worldwide. Through empathy and wisdom from lessons learned, she enlightens and inspires others to find the greater purpose in life's pains and pressures. Morgan's goal is to crush the image and pursuit of perfection by captivating the raw beauty of sincere progress.

FACEBOOK
@modernmorgan

INSTAGRAM
@modernmorgan

TIKTOK
@morganrichardolivier

YOUTUBE
@modernmorgan

the
healing
you
hear

www.morganrichardolivier.com
www.modernmorgan.com

ISBN: 979-8-9857311-7-0

Editor: Carla Dupont
Cover Art: Morgan Richard Olivier
Interior Design: Morgan Richard Olivier
Author Photo: Lori Lyman

www.ingramcontent.com/pod-product-compliance
Lightning Source LLC
Chambersburg PA
CBHW021624120626
46545CB00002B/385